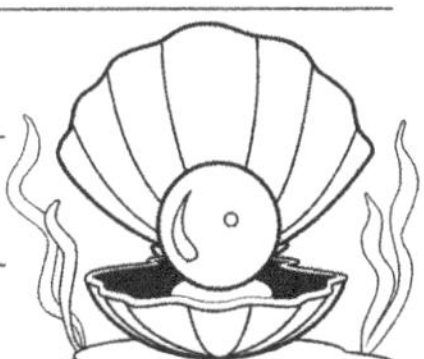

Made in the USA
Monee, IL
11 October 2023

44419879R00057